THE EXTRAORDINARY LIFE OF

# MAHATMA
## GANDHI

First American Edition 2020
Kane Miller, A Division of EDC Publishing

Original edition first published by Penguin Books Ltd, London
Text copyright © Chitra Soundar, 2020
Illustrations copyright © Dàlia Adillon, 2020
The author and the illustrator have asserted their moral rights.

For information contact:
Kane Miller, A Division of EDC Publishing
P.O. Box 470663
Tulsa, OK 74147-0663
**www.kanemiller.com**
**www.usbornebooksandmore.com**

Library of Congress Control Number: 2020937593

Printed and bound in the United States of America
1 2 3 4 5 6 7 8 9 10
ISBN: 978-1-68464-202-1

THE EXTRAORDINARY LIFE OF

# MAHATMA GANDHI

Written by Chitra Soundar
Illustrated by Dàlia Adillon

**Kane Miller**
A DIVISION OF EDC PUBLISHING

MANCHESTER

LONDON

SOUTHAMPTON

PARIS •

JOHANNESBURG •

TOLSTOY FARM

PHOENIX
SETTLEMENT

SOUTH
AFRICA

PIETERMARITZBURG •

DURBAN

# United Kingdom, South Africa & India

EAST
PAKISTAN
(NOW BANGLADESH)

WEST
PAKISTAN

Satyagraha Ashram

Rajkot

INDIA

PORBANDAR

MUMBAI

CALCUTTA
(NOW KOLKATA)

# WHO WAS
# *Mahatma Gandhi?*

# Mahatma Gandhi

was born Mohandas Karamchand Gandhi on October 2, 1869, in the small town of Porbandar on the western coast of India. He grew up to be a leader and activist who changed the course of history.

Mohandas was the **youngest** of four children in his family. He wasn't a bright student or a super sportsman. But he was DILIGENT.

And more importantly he **never followed the crowd** – he didn't do anything just because everyone else was doing it.

DILIGENT: hardworking.

Years later, as a young man and a *lawyer*, he stood up against the RACIAL DISCRIMINATION he and his fellow Indians faced in South Africa.

RACIAL DISCRIMINATION:
unfair treatment of someone or a group of people because of the color of their skin.

When he returned to India, he joined the fight for *Indian independence* from British rule. He led *peaceful protests* against the British and NEGOTIATED on behalf of India and Indians.

NEGOTIATE: discuss a problem until you come to an agreement on what to do.

4

Gandhi was more than a political leader. He was always looking for opportunities to *improve lives*, and he never gave advice that he couldn't follow himself.

lentil

rice

mung

chickpea

Gandhi was really interested in **health**, and he tried out various diets and **treatments** and wrote about them to inform other people. He took comfort in nursing and often volunteered to help ill and old people.

He set up an *ambulance team* during the Boer War in South Africa and again on the western front during the First World War.

Upon joining the fight for India's independence, Gandhi insisted that everyone should be free, including poor and LOW-CASTE people.

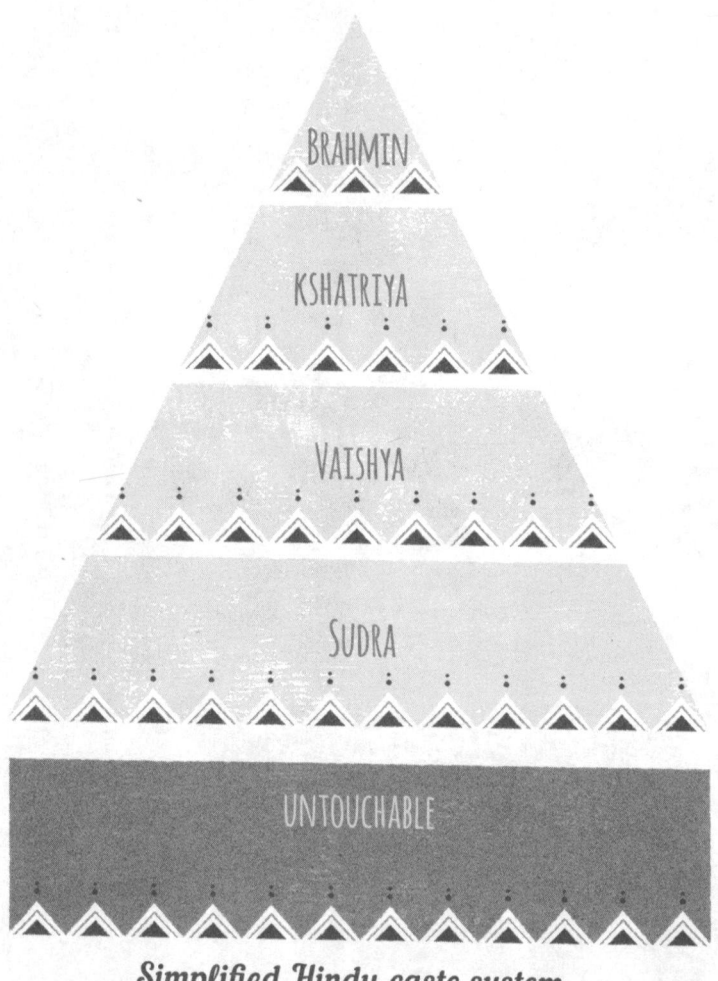

*Simplified Hindu caste system*

## The caste system

More than a thousand years ago, Indian people were divided into groups according to their jobs. Teachers and priests were *Brahmins*, kings and warriors were *Kshatriyas*, merchants and moneylenders were *Vaishyas* and the people who did all the other skilled jobs like carpentry were *Sudras*. The final group was called the *Dalits* or *untouchables*, who were seen as outcasts, and had to clean the streets and do other tasks that were seen as unskilled. These divisions between people were made *official* when India was ruled by Britain. The British told people what jobs to do, and their futures were determined by their *caste ranking*.

Gandhi traveled on foot and in **third-class** railroad cars across the country, meeting people of all **religions, castes and statuses**.

Many people called Gandhi MAHATMA.

MAHATMA: great soul.

But most people simply called him Bapu – father. He was respected widely and was considered the elder of the entire country and an **inspiration** to world leaders.

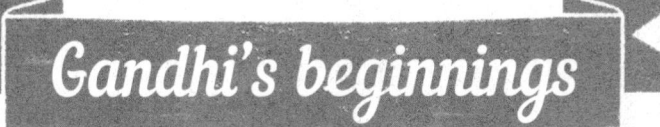

# Gandhi's beginnings

$\mathcal{M}$ohandas was the fourth child of Karamchand Gandhi, who was Diwan (a powerful government official) of Porbandar. The Gandhis belonged to the *Bania caste*, which was made up of merchants.

He was close to his mother, Putlibai, and spent a lot of time with her, listening to stories and helping her around the house.

DID YOU KNOW?
Mohandas played the concertina as a young boy.

12

# Mohandas at school

School wasn't fun for Mohandas. He didn't like multiplication tables and he didn't enjoy sports. When the family moved to Rajkot because of his father's **new job** as a counselor to the leader of Rajkot, Mohandas found it **difficult to adjust** to the new school.

**DID YOU KNOW?**

*Gandhi studied in his mother tongue, Gujarati, until he was about nine, when he switched to reading in English.*

Mohandas was **bookish** and **shy**. He often ran back home just as school finished to avoid mingling with his classmates who sometimes **made fun** of him.

"MY BOOKS
*and*
MY LESSONS
*were my*
SOLE
COMPANIONS."

When he returned from school, his mother would take him to the local **temple** where traveling theaters would perform stories from Hindu EPICS.

Two stories **captured** his heart. One was the story of **King Harishchandra**, who lost his entire family and his kingdom because he refused to break a promise.

EPIC:
a long story about amazing deeds achieved by legendary people.

King Harishchandra seemed to be a good and honest man worthy of going to heaven, but a sage (wise man) named Viswamitra set him a series of tests to find out whether that was true.

The sage lay in wait in one of the king's hunting forests, and when Harishchandra came charging through one day, Viswamitra blamed the king for disturbing his peace. The king was mortified and offered to do anything to make up for disturbing the sage.

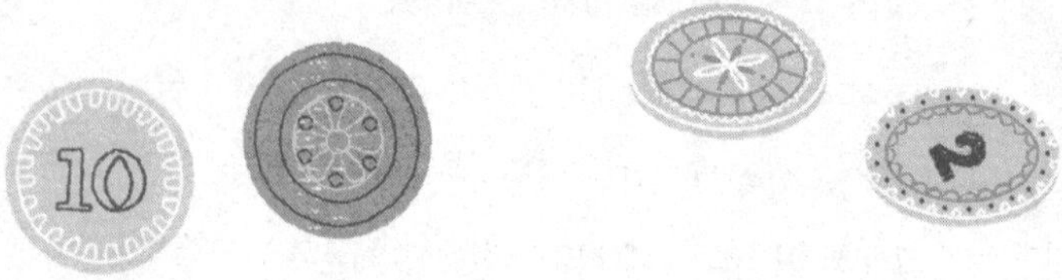

When the sage demanded that Harishchandra give away all his wealth, and then his kingdom, the king readily did so. The sage demanded more gold, and, determined to keep his promise, the king was forced to sell his wife and son as slaves. Eventually the king sold *himself* as a slave to a man who carried out last rites (helping people prepare for death) on the banks of the River Ganga.

The sage went away seeming satisfied. The king's job at the banks of the river was to collect fees for cremation from the families of the dead. One day Harishchandra's wife brought their dead son's body to the docks to be cremated.

The king was overwhelmed with sorrow. But he demanded payment from his wife as was his job. Though everything seemed bleak, the sages and the gods were finally satisfied that the king was indeed an honorable man who kept all his promises. He was invited to heaven.

This story moved Mohandas, who decided that he too would always be *honest* and keep his promises.

## Honesty

*One day, Mohandas was doing a spelling test at school during an inspection. His teacher told him to copy from another student when he didn't know the answer - but he refused. He wouldn't cheat, even if it meant he would fail the test.*

The second story was about **Shravana**, a boy who was so kind that he looked after his blind parents even when he himself was dying.

When he was still a teenager, Mohandas's father became ill and bedridden, and Mohandas remembered the story of Shravana when he helped his mother care for his father every evening after school. Mohandas helped with dressing his father's wounds, grinding up the medicine and massaging his father's legs.

# Married at thirteen

**M**ohandas was a *teenager* in the 1880s, and in those days, where he lived, boys and girls got *married* at a young age. When he was thirteen, Mohandas was married to a quiet yet determined girl called *Kasturba* (affectionately known as Ba). They lived together with Mohandas's parents.

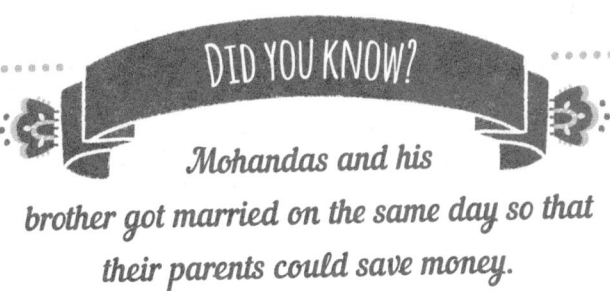

### DID YOU KNOW?

*Mohandas and his brother got married on the same day so that their parents could save money.*

Ba had never been to school and wasn't interested in *studying*, even when Mohandas tried to teach her.

Mohandas was eager to work toward improving the lives of others. After finishing **high school**, he decided to go to **England** to become a BARRISTER.

But his mother didn't want him to go. Eating meat and drinking alcohol were against their *religious principles* as Hindus, and she worried that Mohandas might be *tempted* to do these things in England.

BARRISTER:
a type of lawyer in the UK and Commonwealth.

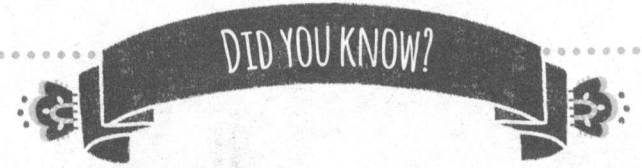

DID YOU KNOW?

*Four of the world's major religions were born in India: Hinduism, Buddhism, Jainism and Sikhism.*

Mohandas would also have to leave behind his young wife and their **new baby boy**, Harilal.

But Mohandas was **determined** to go. With the help of his older brother and a monk at the temple, he made a **promise** to his mother that he would not eat meat or drink alcohol while he was in England. She **blessed** him by giving him a garland of beads to remind him of his promise, and Mohandas set off for England.

# Life in England

Before Mohandas boarded a ship to Southampton, he had never used *knives and forks* to eat. He did not speak English fluently and had never lived anywhere but home. Wearing unfamiliar clothes, he went on an unfamiliar journey toward an *unfamiliar destination*.

# "I was quite UNACCUSTOMED to talking English."

When the ship docked in England, Mohandas felt instantly out of place. The weather was cold and **vegetarian food** was hard to find. Often he ate only porridge for breakfast, and plain spinach, bread and jam for lunch and dinner.

But he was **determined** to fit in. He bought himself a suit from a tailor's shop on Bond Street, London, and tried to learn dancing and how to play the piano.

## Dancing disaster

*After six dancing lessons, Mohandas couldn't follow the rhythm and movement well enough, and gave up!*

To save money, he **walked** wherever he could. He kept a record of every single penny he spent, and continued to do this all his life.

On one of these walks, he found the *London Vegetarian Society*, which started his lifelong interest in diet and health. He studied hard at *University College, London*, in order to become a barrister.

While in England, Gandhi also studied different religions. He discussed and **debated** religion with friends, and always remained true to his belief in a **higher power**, or God.

Finally he *passed his exams* and was CALLED TO THE BAR on June 10, 1891.

He set sail for home two days after that. His goals were accomplished!

When someone is CALLED TO THE BAR it means they have passed all the tests and become qualified to work as a lawyer in court in the UK and Commonwealth.

When he returned home, he found out that his mother had passed away while he had been in London. Mohandas was *devastated*. But he hid his grief and started a *new chapter* in his life as a barrister.

# A father and a lawyer

When Mohandas returned to India, he enjoyed spending time with his *four-year-old* son, Harilal, and his nephews.

But soon he had to leave them all in Porbandar so that he could set up an **office** in Bombay.

Being a lawyer turned out to be even **more difficult** than he had expected. Mohandas was **terrified** of speaking in public.

His first case wasn't a big one, but he felt **intimidated** by it. He panicked and ran out of the courtroom, leaving his client stranded.

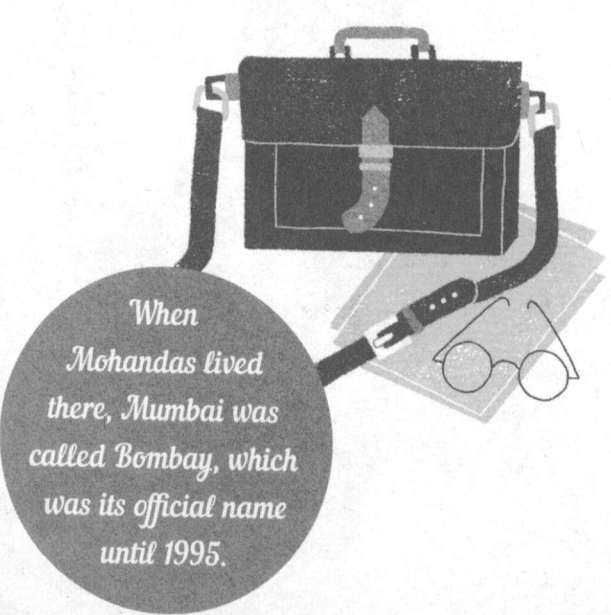

When Mohandas lived there, Mumbai was called Bombay, which was its official name until 1995.

"I HASTENED
FROM THE COURT,
*not knowing
whether my client*
WON OR LOST HER CASE,
*but I was*
ASHAMED OF MYSELF,
*and decided not to
take up any more cases*
UNTIL I HAD
COURAGE ENOUGH
*to conduct them.*"

This only made Mohandas more determined to succeed.

A few months later an opportunity to work in **South Africa** unexpectedly arose. He was offered a job helping a **merchant** with a legal case. He accepted readily. Little did he know that this job was the start of his **lifetime** of work and achievements.

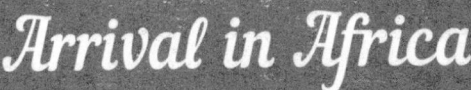

# Arrival in Africa

**W**hen Mohandas Gandhi moved to South Africa it was still a British COLONY and there were some disagreements between all of the different communities that lived there.

**COLONY:** a country that is under the political control of a different country.

## The British Empire

*Places all over the world became part of the British Empire when the British Army and navy invaded, and established control over the native people.*

In South Africa, the British had divided their rule into four colonies: Natal, Transvaal, the Orange River Colony and Cape Colony. People of color living in these places had hardly any rights.

transvaal

orange
reiver
colony

natal
colony

south
atlantic
ocean

cape colony

indian ocea

The **wealthy** people in South Africa – the people who owned land and diamond mines – were the British and the Boers (the original Dutch settlers from Europe). Life for native black Africans was challenging, and they faced a lot of discrimination.

**Laborers** from colonies outside Africa, mostly from India and Indonesia, were brought in to work on the farms and mines.

These laborers paid high taxes and lived in **poor conditions**. Some merchants and shopkeepers had come on the journey too, and they set up shops and shipping businesses.

Gandhi arrived in 1893 as a **proud** young barrister, only to find that Indians in South Africa were often **mistreated** and called insulting names.

On his first day of work, he went to the court in Natal. He was wearing a **turban**, which was traditional for a man of his status in Indian society.

"MY TURBAN STAYED WITH ME practically until the end of my stay IN SOUTH AFRICA."

But Indian men in South Africa had **very low status.** The judge ordered him to remove his turban, which **angered** Gandhi. He refused, and then wrote to the newspapers about the outrage.

Soon he left for Pretoria to oversee the court case. But that journey too turned out to be full of **trouble**.

# On the way to Pretoria

Gandhi bought a *first-class ticket* for the train from Natal to Pretoria. But during the journey one of the white passengers **complained** and said that he should be removed from the first-class car. Gandhi refused. The guard pushed Gandhi off the train at the next station and threw his luggage after him.

The train left and Gandhi was **alone**, cold and hungry on the platform in Pietermaritzburg. He **brooded** over the event all night in the waiting room.

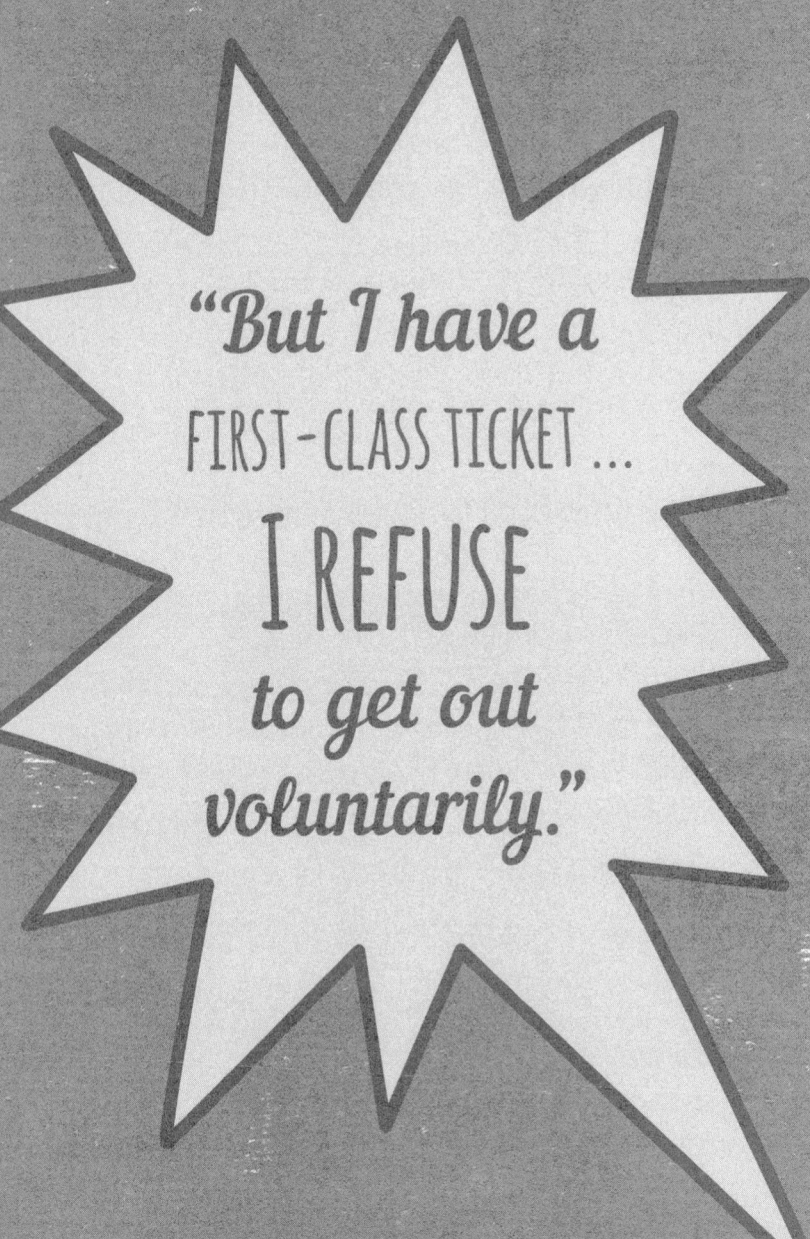

Many Indians came to speak to him the next day as he waited for his train. They told him about the **hardships** they suffered in South Africa. Gandhi decided that something needed to be done.

A plaque has been put up at the station today that reads:

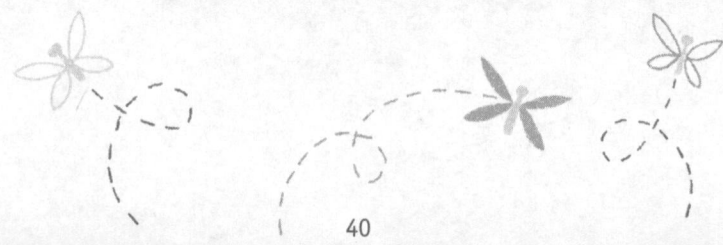

### ◀ Mahatma Gandhi ▶

In the vicinity of this plaque M.K. Gandhi was evicted from a first-class compartment on the night of 7 June 1893. This incident changed the course of his life. He took up the fight against racial oppression. His active non-violence started from that date.

# Making changes

Back in Pretoria, Gandhi wanted to MOBILIZE a group that understood the problem. He requested a *meeting* of all the Indians living there so he could talk about their hardships.

Seeking to empower other Indians, he offered *English lessons* to traders and merchants, and walked many miles to do so.

MOBILIZE: organize people to work or take action together.

A year after he arrived in South Africa, Gandhi's **court case** was over. He and his client had won.

At his **farewell party**, Gandhi noticed a small article in the newspaper. It said that the government in South Africa was considering **removing** Indians from the voters' roll (the register of names).

## Unfair system

ballot box

*At this time, black South Africans did not have the right to vote in elections in South Africa. If Indians were removed from the voters' roll, they too wouldn't be able to vote.*

Gandhi wanted the Indians all around him at his party to **protest** against the decision. They in turn asked him to **stay and fight** for them.

Gandhi agreed. That night, instead of enjoying the party, they formed a **committee** to fight against the proposed law. Gandhi wrote a PETITION, which was copied out by hand by many volunteers through the night.

PETITION:
a written document requesting something from an important person or group. The more signatures there are, the more powerful the petition.

Mahatma Gandhi

The committee formed that night was eventually turned into the *Natal Indian Congress*, which fought for the rights of Indians in South Africa.

The fight took *longer* than they had expected. Three years later, Gandhi returned to India, intending to bring his family back to *South Africa*. During his short time in his home country, he met with *influential leaders* to gain support for the cause. He wrote *petitions* and gave *speeches*.

In December 1896, Gandhi and his family *sailed to South Africa* aboard the SS *Courland*.

While Gandhi had been in India, the South African government and the white people who lived in South Africa had turned extremely **anti-Indian**. The ships from India carrying Gandhi and his family, as well as many other Indians, were **stopped in the port** and the government refused to let anyone ashore. At first they said it was for QUARANTINE – the doctors wanted to make sure that no one had the **plague**.

**QUARANTINE:** keeping certain people completely separate from others to avoid the spread of diseases.

But Gandhi knew it wasn't just that. The local white people were *protesting* and had convinced the government that the Indians should not be let in – especially not Gandhi.

Gandhi *refused* to let the ships be turned away. He *argued* with officials that he had a right to enter the country because he was a RESIDENT of South Africa.

RESIDENT:
someone with the legal right to live in a certain country.

Eventually, after more than three weeks, the government had **no more excuses** and couldn't prevent Gandhi and the rest of the Indians from entering the country.

But some angry locals were waiting at the docks and when Gandhi stepped onto the shore, they **attacked** him. Even though he was badly wounded, he refused to **press charges** against his attackers, which surprised many South Africans.

# "I have NO ANGER against them."

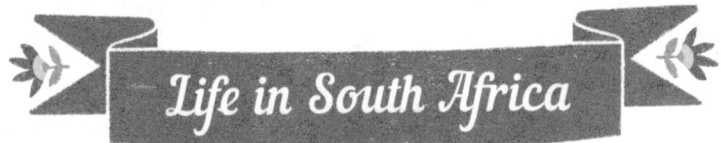

# Life in South Africa

The Gandhi family eventually settled into a *routine*.

 ## The Gandhi family

*Gandhi and Kasturba had four sons –
Harilal and Manilal, born in 1888 and 1892
in India, and Ramdas and Devdas,
born in 1897 and 1900 in South Africa.*

Gandhi was kept busy as a lawyer, but he felt that just doing his job and looking after his family *wasn't enough* to live a good life. He wanted to do something more for *other people*.

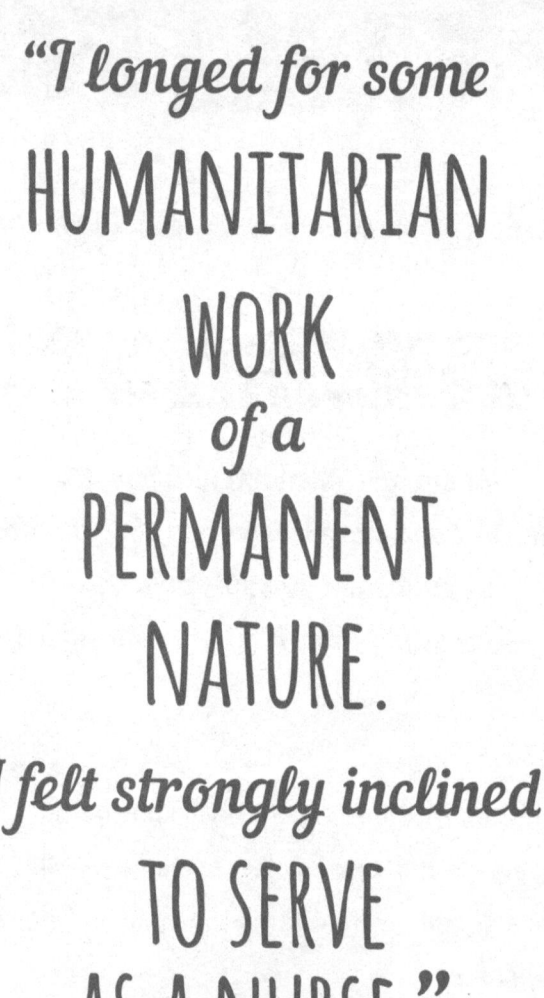

"I longed for some **HUMANITARIAN WORK** *of a* **PERMANENT NATURE.** *I felt strongly inclined* **TO SERVE AS A NURSE.**"

As well as serving as a **nurse** in a local hospital after work, he homeschooled his children, **washed and ironed** his own clothes, **cleaned** the house and the toilets and cut his own hair.

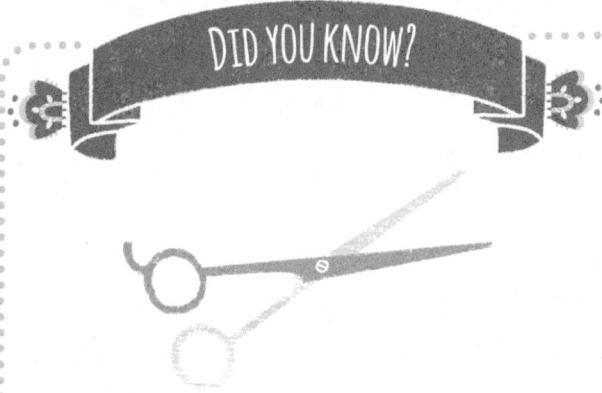

## DID YOU KNOW?

*In those days, white barbers refused to cut the hair of men of color. Gandhi did a decent job of cutting the front of his hair, but at the back it was rather uneven, and many of his friends made fun of him!*

Even though the unfair law that Gandhi *fought against* was imposed by the British, when **war broke out** between the Boers (the Dutch-speaking settlers in South Africa) and the British, Gandhi *supported the British.*

He believed that if Indians wanted to be **citizens of the British Empire**, then they should do their bit to help Britain. He set up an **ambulance team** and worked for many days caring for the wounded soldiers and native people.

 *Gandhi at war*

*Later in life, when he was negotiating with Britain, Gandhi offered Indian troops to fight in the First and Second World Wars to support the British. Those who knew him as a peace-loving person were surprised every time he chose to serve in the war.*

Even while he was still a *young lawyer*, he was looking out for the *welfare* of the community he belonged to. When a terrible plague broke out in 1902 Gandhi *cared for the sick*. He was always talking about the *importance of hygiene* in daily life and *petitioned* the South African government for *running water* and proper drainage for poor workers.

In 1903 Gandhi started a *newspaper* called the *Indian Opinion*. It was printed not just in English but in *Gujarati*, *Hindi* and *Tamil*, which were three of the languages Indians spoke across the four colonies of South Africa. He wrote many of the original articles in Gujarati himself.

He also wrote **books and articles** on many topics that interested him – food, health, and the issues he came across in his life. In 1904 Gandhi and his friend Mr. West bought a place called Tolstoy Farm in *Phoenix*, near Johannesburg, far away from their current office, and decided to move the newspaper there.

The residents of the farm lived on an allowance of **£3 a month** (about $15) and strove to do everything they could **by hand**. Even the *printing press* was fully hand operated.

Four years later, Gandhi decided to go **back to India**. He promised his friends in South Africa that he would **return** if they needed him.

# Satyagraha

Back in India, Gandhi spent a month with **Gopal Krishna Gokhale**, a math professor and a leader who fought for SOCIAL REFORM and *self-rule*.

SOCIAL REFORM: movement that seeks to change rules so that everyday life can become better.

## Self-rule

India was a part of the British Empire, but many Indians wanted self-rule, also known as **swaraj**, instead. This meant independence from a colonizing country.

When Gokhale urged Gandhi to join the fight for *freedom*, Gandhi pointed out that he had no knowledge of life in India, having lived mainly in England and South Africa since he grew up.

Gokhale suggested that Gandhi *travel around India* and meet ordinary people. Then he would understand their lives and be able to speak out for them. With a single cloth bag full of his belongings and a *third-class* train ticket, Gandhi set off. Gokhale then advised him to start his law practice in Bombay and Gandhi returned.

But just as he was getting started, his friends in **South Africa** called for help. He left his family in Bombay and returned to South Africa.

While he was away this time, the government of South Africa had passed **even more laws** to limit the freedom of Indian people. They had created the **Asiatic Department**, which decided whether Indians (and other Asians such as Chinese people) could **travel** from one colony to another. This made life very **difficult** for Indians in South Africa.

Then came the Asiatic Registration Act of the Transvaal Colony, or the BLACK ACT.

 ## The Black Act

*This was a law that stated every male citizen of Asian origin must register and get an identification card that showed their fingerprints. If they were found without their ID card, they could be jailed, beaten or even deported.*

At first Gandhi and his friends in the Natal Indian Congress protested against it.

Then Gandhi negotiated a **compromise** with General Smuts, who was the leader of Transvaal. If Gandhi and the other Indians registered **willingly**, the general would REPEAL the Black Act. But General Smuts didn't keep that promise.

REPEAL: cancel.

Indians gathered in **peaceful protest** and burned all their registration certificates. Gandhi called this peaceful protest "SATYAGRAHA."

SATYAGRAHA: the determination to fight for the truth.

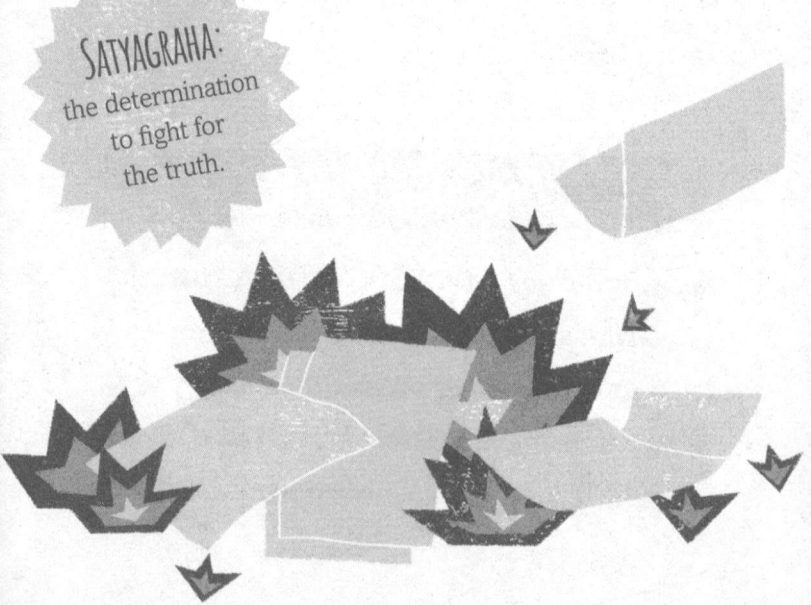

The most important principle of satyagraha was
*ahimsa* (nonviolence).

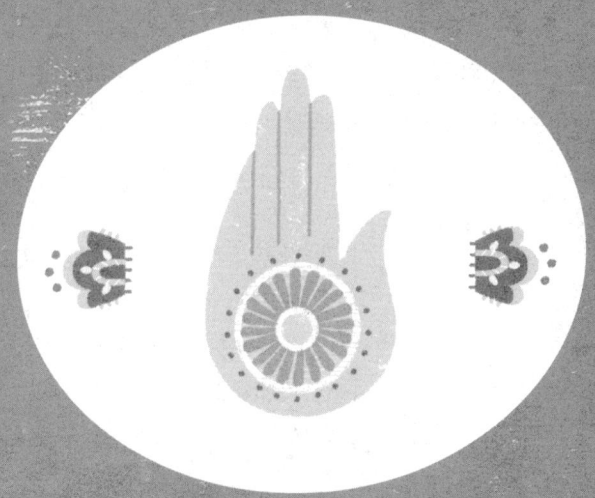

"HATE THE SIN *and not* THE SINNER."

The participants of satyagraha allowed themselves to be **arrested**. They did not *fight back* if they were beaten. But they also *refused to stop protesting*.

Soon, the government imposed an **unfair tax** on some laborers. The protesters continued standing up and using *satyagraha*.

Kasturba Gandhi led a group of women protesters and was arrested. Miners soon joined the movement by *leaving their work*, which caused huge losses for the South African companies they worked for.

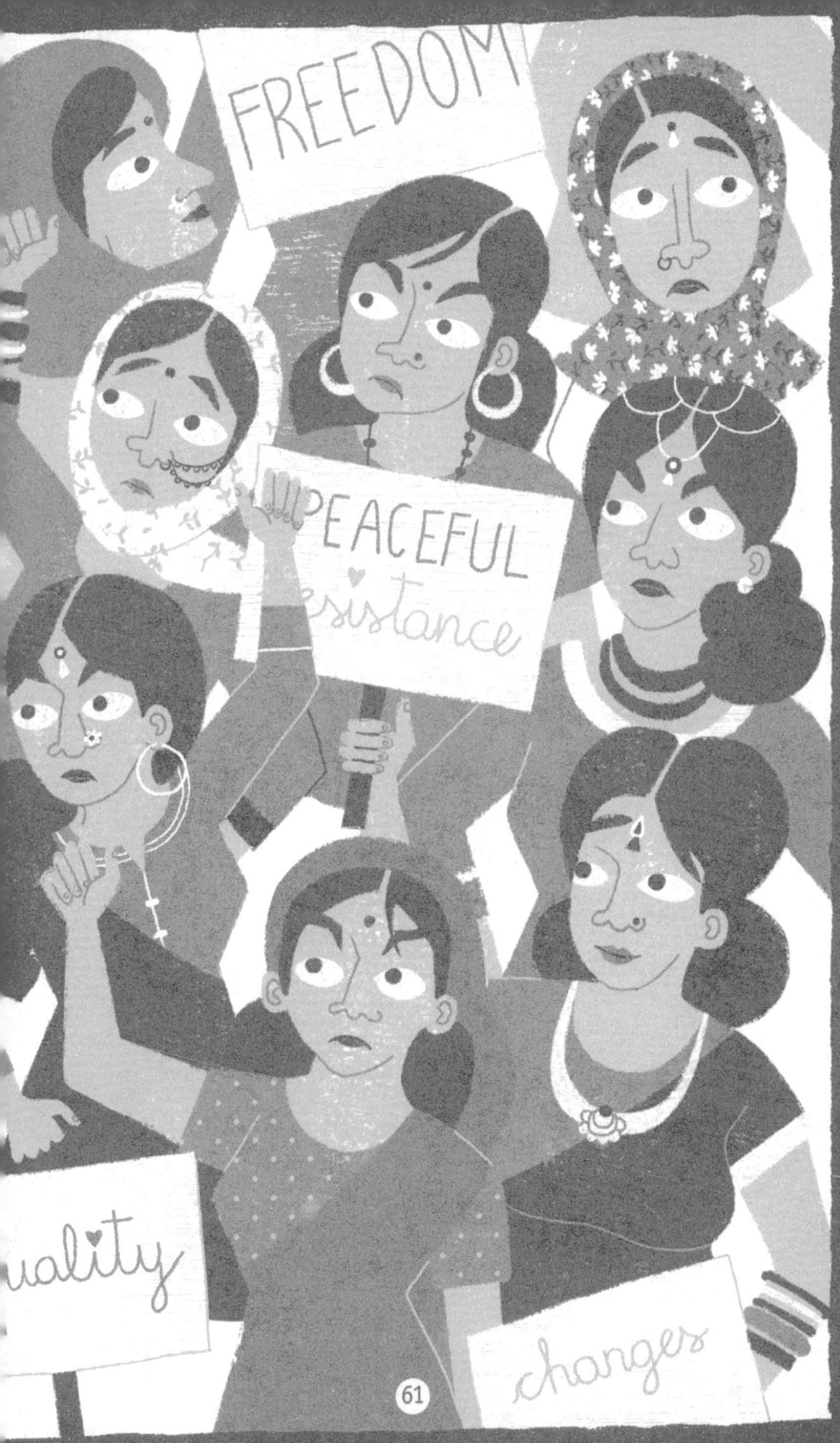
FREEDOM
PEACEFUL
esistance
uality
changes

Prisons were filling up with peaceful protesters. Eventually General Smuts agreed to set up a committee to investigate the protests. This **committee** agreed with the Indians that many of the laws had been ***illegally introduced***.

In 1914 Gandhi's satyagraha succeeded in ***repealing the laws***, and Gandhi decided to leave South Africa.

# Satyagraha in India

When Gandhi finally returned to India in 1915, many of his family and friends came with him. So he set up a settlement called SATYAGRAHA ASHRAM. In 1917 the Ashram moved to the bank of the River Sabarmati and became known as Sabarmati Ashram. Just like they had done in South Africa, Gandhi and his followers grew their own food and lived to serve others.

ASHRAM:
a community or village where people who believe the same things live and work together.

lentil

rice

chickpea

mung

During this time, Gandhi helped out in the community and also participated in the national independence struggle led by the Indian National Congress.

British landlords in Champaran, a region in the foothills of **the *Himalayan mountains***, were forcing Indian farmers to grow indigo, a plant that was used to create blue dyes. But the landlords had stopped buying indigo, so the farmers couldn't sell it anywhere, and had no money even for food.

Gandhi and his followers went to live in Champaran, where they protested against the British landlords on the side of the farmers. It wasn't long before the landlords lost their case in court and the farmers were COMPENSATED.

COMPENSATE: give money to someone to make up for them having lost something.

After the **success** of Champaran, Gandhi went to help **mill workers** in Ahmedabad protest against **unfair pay**, and then **farmers** in Kheda who were being asked to **pay taxes** even when their harvests had failed.

## The charka

When the British ruled India, they bought cotton cheaply from India and shipped it to England, where it was made into cloth in big mills. Then they sold the cloth back to Indians at high prices.

Gandhi believed that India should make its own cloth and not have to rely on Britain. He suggested that the workers in India make cloth by using a kind of spinning wheel called a charka. The charka soon became the symbol of self-reliance.

Even when he was in meetings or traveling, Gandhi *spun cotton* to prove to people that it was possible to *move away* from relying on the British.

The hand-spun cotton was called **khadi** and it became the **symbol** of the Satyagraha movement. People who were fighting for India's freedom from British rule wore homespun khadi and **burned** their British clothes.

# The Indian caste system in action

$S$ome people of the upper castes in India **mistreated** the people who were outcastes (known as *achuth* in Hindi or "untouchables").

## → Being an "untouchable" ←

*In those days, the untouchables (also known as Dalits) weren't allowed to draw water from the same well as other people because it was believed their use would pollute the water. They couldn't enter temples or other people's homes. Their children couldn't go to school - and so their misery continued for generation after generation.*

Gandhi thought the system was unfair and he was upset by the *suffering* it caused. He often criticized the ORTHODOX Hindus who followed these *customs*.

**ORTHODOX:** traditional, long established.

Gandhi didn't like the word *achuth* and so instead he called the Dalits "Harijans," or "the people of God." He believed that Indians who complained about how the British treated them yet kept treating their fellow Indians badly were HYPOCRITES.

**HYPOCRITE:** someone whose actions are the opposite of the things that they say.

Gandhi opened his ashram to Dalits. And whenever he traveled from one city to another, he stayed in the slums with them.

Gandhi went on a thirteen-day FAST to encourage the Hindus to agree on voting rights for the Dalits.

**FAST:** when someone refuses to eat, often as a means to draw attention to a particular issue.

**"I want to allow**

# NO

## DIFFERENTIATION

*between the son of*

## A WEAVER,

*of an*

## AGRICULTURIST

*and of a*

## SCHOOLMASTER."

All across the country, Hindu temples opened their doors to Dalits. **Thousands** of important high-caste Hindus spent time with the Dalits in public, showing Gandhi that they fully supported his fight for **equality**. Villages and towns allowed Dalits to draw water from the public wells, and schools were opened to Dalit children.

## Ongoing problems

*It's important to remember that caste prejudice still exists in India. While Gandhi's fasting opened the doors to temples, schools and homes, it didn't always open people's minds. But it was an important step toward changing Hindu society. Later, when India eventually got independence from the British, everyone, no matter their caste, was given equal status by the first law minister of free India, B. R. Ambedkar, who had campaigned for the freedom of the Dalits.*

# United religions

*I*n many parts of India, Hindus and Muslims lived next to each other, had *similar traditions* and took part in each other's *religious festivals*. But there were far more Hindus than Muslims, Sikhs or Christians in India.

When the British came to rule India, they encouraged *suspicion* between the religions. They tried to fill the Muslims with fear that the Hindus would never treat them equally, and helped Muslims set up the Muslim League, which aimed to safeguard the rights of Indian Muslims. Later, the British even tried to divide the eastern state of *Bengal* into two separate states – one for Muslims and the other for Hindus.

Gandhi believed in ***treating people equally***, no matter their religion. With satyagraha he had united people from all religions and backgrounds.

 ## The partition

*The British had tried to partition Bengal once before, in 1905. But people had protested, and the state was reunited in 1911. Now, the British were helping the Muslim League to propose separation all over again.*

Gandhi and others strongly believed that the lack of Hindu–Muslim unity was an Indian problem and they could solve it ***after the British left***. But Mohammad Ali Jinnah, a barrister who was the leader of the Muslim League, wanted the British to sort it out before they left the country.

As the struggle for ***Indian independence*** continued, the Muslim League called for a ***separate state*** for Muslims. They wanted East Bengal and West Punjab to be united to form a new country called ***Pakistan***.

west pakistan

india

east pakistan

While these conversations were happening between the Muslim League and Hindu leaders, fiery speeches were made and *riots broke out*. People *mistrusted* their own neighbors and fought with each other. Gandhi went to troubled areas, stayed with Muslim friends and fasted until the Hindus and Muslims sat together to share prayers from both religions, eat meals together and discuss their issues.

## Mahatma

Gandhi was referred to as Mahatma (a great soul) toward the end of his time in South Africa. When he came to India, the title followed him there and many leaders called him the Mahatma.

# The fight for Indian independence

The British had agreed that if India helped them in the First World War by giving money and soldiers, they would grant DOMINION STATUS to India, just like South Africa. However, after the war was over the British backed out of this promise.

**DOMINION STATUS:** permission for a country to set up its own government and rule itself.

"I feel sure that nothing less than a DEFINITE VISION OF HOME RULE to be realized in the SHORTEST POSSIBLE TIME will satisfy the Indian people."

The Indian people felt **betrayed**. Many of them were upset with Gandhi for trusting the British government. They urged him to lead a **massive protest.**

Gandhi suggested that India should observe a HARTAL. The British would have to **take notice.**

HARTAL:
a strike that lasts all day, when shops, offices and schools are closed.

"Let all the PEOPLE OF INDIA, therefore, SUSPEND THEIR BUSINESS on that day and OBSERVE THE DAY as one of FASTING AND PRAYER."

On April 6, 1919, people in Bombay gathered on the *shores of the Arabian Sea* for peaceful prayer and fasting. Gandhi was *impressed* with how India had come together *peacefully* to protest.

But in some neighborhoods, the protests turned into *clashes* between the police and the protesters. And on April 12, in the holy city of *Amritsar* in Punjab, General Dyer, an important officer of the British Army, *banned* public gatherings and protests, even peaceful ones.

The next day, the people of Amritsar gathered to *celebrate the start of spring* at a festival called *Vasantha Panchami*. They congregated in Jallianwala Bagh, a square surrounded by buildings. There happened to be some protest speeches going on in the square, too. Over *ten thousand people* had gathered.

General Dyer **blocked all the exits** from the public square. He didn't give the people a **warning** or a **chance to leave.** He ordered his officers to shoot at the people.

Hundreds of people were killed by the bullets and many **jumped into a public well** to escape the attack. The entire country was **devastated**.

Mahatma Gandhi was shocked. He decided that he would no longer support India's self-rule under the British Empire. He wanted *Poorna Swaraj* – **complete independence** from Great Britain.

# "POORNA SWARAJ...

*because it is as much*
## FOR THE PRINCE
## AS FOR THE PEASANT,
*as much for the rich landowner as for the landless tiller of the soil,*

AS MUCH FOR THE HINDUS AS FOR THE MUSALMANS (MUSLIMS), *as much for Parsis and Christians as for the Jains, Jews and Sikhs,* IRRESPECTIVE OF ANY DISTINCTION OF CASTE *or creed or status in life."*

# Inspirational leader

**G**andhi firmly believed that the only way to drive **Britain out of India** was to **peacefully** refuse to co-operate with their rulers. India was large, and in order for it to work, his message needed to reach every town and every small village.

*"An India*
# AWAKENED
# AND FREE
*has a message of*
# PEACE AND
# GOODWILL
*to a groaning world."*

Gandhi traveled on trains and by foot, all the way across the country, teaching *satyagraha*, his nonviolent noncooperation. Many people quit their jobs at this time and volunteered to help *spread his message*. He inspired people to do their bit even if it was in a small way, whether it was not paying their taxes to the British government or wearing Indian handmade khadi instead of store-bought British cotton.

But the government wasn't paying attention. The VICEROY didn't even want to grant India self-rule.

While Gandhi was traveling across India, he wanted to test whether the people of India were ready to fight *peacefully* for independence. He launched a small *peaceful protest* in Bardoli. But violence broke out anyway.

VICEROY: the most powerful officer of the British Empire in India.

"SATYAGRAHA
IS GENTLE,
it never wounds.
IT MUST NOT BE
the result of
ANGER OR MALICE...
It was conceived as
A COMPLETE
SUBSTITUTE
FOR VIOLENCE."

Even though he had *peaceful intentions*, the government didn't like the fact that Gandhi had started a protest. They *blamed him* for the violence and he was sent to prison for *six years*, which he accepted without complaint.

But Gandhi became ill in jail and had to have an operation. In the end he was released from prison four years early. Discouraged by the violence in the disobedience movement, he still *refused to fight* for freedom. He wanted to spend his time uniting Hindus and Muslims. He even fasted for twenty-one days in the house of a Muslim friend to show Hindus and Muslims how to treat each other as family.

While Gandhi was in prison, the protest movement *fizzled out*. There was no one to lead the struggle in his absence. He felt like no one was listening to his teachings of peaceful objection.

When he was released from prison in 1924 he *retreated* to his ashram and spent a year writing and thinking about how to carry on. Every Monday during this year he kept a *silent fast*, when he wouldn't *speak or eat* at all.

"Try to understand

# THE

# OPPONENT'S

# VIEWPOINT

and, if we

cannot accept it,

# RESPECT IT

as fully as we expect

him to respect ours."

In December 1928 Gandhi, along with the political party the Indian National Congress, gave Britain an ULTIMATUM: if Britain did not *willingly* give them dominion status by December 31, 1929, the Indians would *take it anyway*.

The British government *ignored* the deadline of December 1929. And so Gandhi and the Indian National Congress *declared that India was free*.

## ULTIMATUM:

when someone makes a demand followed by a threat if the demand isn't met.

# The Dandi March

It was difficult to know how to carry out India's declaration of freedom – how could the people of India tell the British they refused to follow the laws of the British Empire?

 ## The Salt Act of 1930

India is surrounded by seas on three sides, so people often gathered salt from the ocean and sold it. The British Empire's Salt Act of 1930 said that the sea salt belonged to Britain and if Indians took it, they had to pay a salt tax (extra money to the British government).

On March 12, 1930, at ten past six in the morning, **Gandhi set out on a journey**. He wanted to **peacefully challenge** the British Empire – and he wanted to use the Salt Act to do so.

Thousands of Indians joined Gandhi's march, and he led them on the **journey by foot**, covering 240 miles in weeks. People watching showered the marchers with **flowers and coins** to show their support. Finally Gandhi reached the coastal village of **Dandi** on April 5, 1930, with thousands of supporters right behind him.

Gandhi bent down and **scooped up seawater** in his palms, poured it on the beach and **picked up the salt** left by the waves. His actions **broke the law** because this salt had not been gathered and sold by the British.

### DID YOU KNOW?

*On the day he reached Dandi, Gandhi hadn't eaten salt in many years. He had given it up when he lived in South Africa. He gathered salt to prove to his entire country how important it was to defy British laws.*

*Across India*, in every village and town, people started to go on their own salt marches. The British government **arrested thousands of people.** But that only **inspired** others to join the protests. Gandhi was **arrested** again.

Gandhi's supporters understood by now the power of **nonviolence**. They did not **fight back** when the police beat them. They **marched forward**, sang patriotic songs and continued to be peaceful. They were **no longer afraid** of their colonial masters, the British.

All across the world, empires were being disbanded. Many people in India were fighting for independence, including Gandhi and his followers. It was the beginning of the end of British rule in India.

# The fight continues

The British government was **alarmed** at the success of this peaceful resistance. Prisons were *filling up* and there was no sign that the protests were going to die down. They decided to discuss self-rule, with key Indian and British leaders present.

Gandhi represented the Indian National Congress and he *sailed to London*. Though it was cold and wet when he arrived, Gandhi still wore his familiar shawl and dhoti (a long piece of cotton tied around the waist, covering most of the legs) and didn't even put on a jacket.

He **refused** to stay at the fancy hotel that the British government was paying for. He chose to stay in East London in a *poor neighborhood*.

*Even when Gandhi was invited to meet King George V, he refused to wear a suit. This didn't impress the king at all!*

While he was in England, Gandhi visited Manchester and met with the workers in the mills. He explained to them why he encouraged people to **burn British clothes** and instead wear homespun Indian cotton. The mill workers listened to his words and didn't get upset at all.

But the conference in London **didn't solve anything** for India. The British government wanted to SEGREGATE voters by their caste and religion, and this angered Gandhi.

**SEGREGATE:** separate and keep apart from each other.

Gandhi returned home **disappointed and worried** about what was to come.

# The Second World War

*T*he **Second World War** broke out in 1939. Britain and its allies were fighting FASCIST Nazi Germany, Italy and Japan.

**FASCIST:**
someone who believes that one ruler should have complete power, and that everyone who disagrees with that ruler should be forcibly silenced.

The leaders of India offered to *support the British troops* in the war, in return for their freedom as a country.

## British hypocrisy

*The Indians pointed out that it was hypocritical of Britain to fight the fascists in Europe when they themselves were trying to control countries like India.*

But Winston Churchill, who was the British prime minister at the time, *refused to give independence* to India. So in 1942, Indian leaders, including Gandhi, launched the *Quit India movement.*

# QUIT INDIA

The Quit India movement was created when a British mission called the Cripps Mission tried to give partial dominion status to India in return for full Indian cooperation and support in the war effort. Gandhi gave a speech in Bombay in August 1942, which invited Indians to oppose this by using nonviolence to gain total freedom from the British.

"I SHALL WORK FOR AN INDIA in which the poorest shall feel that it is THEIR COUNTRY ... an India in which there shall be NO HIGH CLASS AND LOW CLASS OF PEOPLE; an India in which all communities shall live IN PERFECT HARMONY."

Mahatma Gandhi, Kasturba Gandhi and many others were **arrested for protesting** against the government.

While in prison, Kasturba became ill. She wanted an **Ayurvedic doctor** (a doctor who practiced Hindu medicine). But the government **did not allow** her to have one for many days. Finally, when the doctor came, it was too late.

Kasturba died in Mahatma Gandhi's arms **inside the prison**.

# Partition

*I*ndia has always been a country of many languages, customs, foods and religions. As in any **big country**, this causes some problems.

The British rulers had in many ways **emphasized people's differences** when it came to caste and religion.

Gandhi **objected** to the idea of a separate state for Muslims. He even offered Mohammad Jinnah the important job of first **prime minister** of India, but this solution did not satisfy everybody involved.

The Hindus feared that the Muslims would *evict* them. The Muslims feared that the Hindus would *attack* them. So in many villages, especially in *Bengal*, people clashed with one another. Neighbors turned on each other and *fights broke out*. There were *riots* across the country between Hindus and Muslims.

Mahatma Gandhi went to Bengal and *fasted for many days*. He refused to break his fast until the people put down their weapons. Many riots were *calmed* by Gandhi's peaceful actions. But the problem was *too big* for one person to solve. One man, however great, couldn't be heard over the *roar* of the many who were being forced to MIGRATE across the borders.

MIGRATE:
move from one place to another, usually in large numbers.

It was agreed that in 1947, **when Britain left India**, the British would help **divide the country** into two – India and Pakistan. Pakistan would get the two states with the **highest population of Muslims** – one in the west and the other in the east.

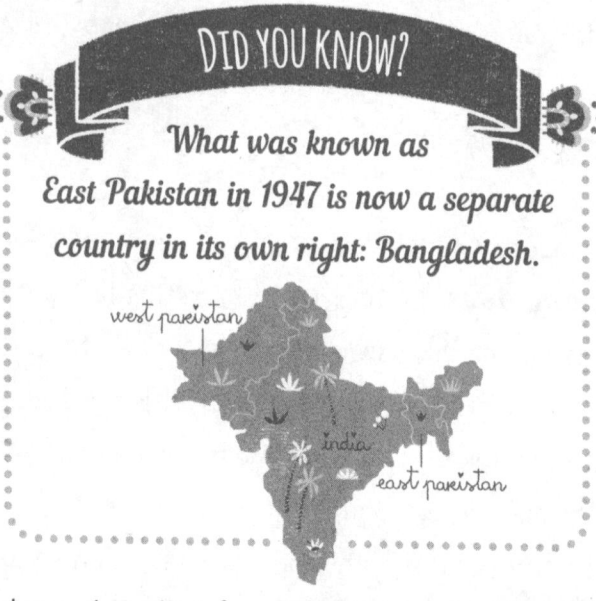

## DID YOU KNOW?

*What was known as East Pakistan in 1947 is now a separate country in its own right: Bangladesh.*

west pakistan

india

east pakistan

Hindus and Muslims **hurried** to be on the right side of the border. This caused much pain, anguish, loss of land, divided families and more. **More than a million people** lost their lives as they moved between the border of India and Pakistan in the east and the west. The terrible and violent nature of the **partition** still affects the relationship between India and Pakistan to this day.

 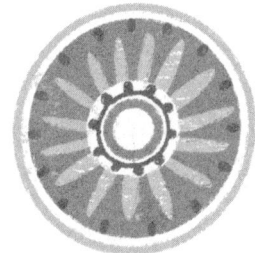 

# Indian independence

On August 15, 1947, Britain passed the *Indian Independence Act*, which declared that India was free. As the country celebrated, Mahatma Gandhi was not in the capital city of *Delhi*. He wasn't giving speeches. He was fasting in Calcutta to stop the *Hindu-Muslim riots* that had broken out again.

Soon India started functioning as a *new country*. Jawaharlal Nehru became the first *prime minister of India*.

Mahatma Gandhi *didn't want* a government job. By now he had *retired* for a life of *prayers and peace*. At that time he was living in *Delhi* in Birla House, which is now called Birla Mandir.

January 30, 1948, started like any other day. When the time came for evening prayers, Mahatma Gandhi came out of his room, helped by his grandnieces. He was a little bit late, and he disliked being late. So he *hurried* to the platform where he sat to *lead the prayers*.

The crowds *chanted his name*. Many came forward to *pay their respects*. But one man in particular *pushed through the crowd* and fell down at Gandhi's feet, which is customary in India where people show respect to the elders by touching their feet.

But this man, *Nathuram Godse*, was a Hindu EXTREMIST who **blamed** Mahatma Gandhi for the partition. He shot Gandhi in the chest three times with a handgun.

EXTREMIST:
someone whose political or religious views are dangerously extreme.

DID YOU KNOW?
January 30, the anniversary of Gandhi's death, is celebrated as Martyrs' Day in India.

*Mohandas Gandhi* fell to the ground. His last words were "Hai Ram," the name of his God. Only five and a half months after India's independence, the country lost its Mahatma.

The custom for Hindus was that the **oldest son** cremated the body of his father. But Gandhi and his eldest son, Harilal, were ESTRANGED.

ESTRANGED: turned away from each other, no longer in contact.

Gandhi's second son, Manilal, was in *South Africa* and couldn't reach Delhi in time. So Gandhi was cremated by his third son, *Ramdas Gandhi*, alongside his fourth son, *Devdas Gandhi*. They were surrounded by friends, family, Congress leaders, statesmen and millions of Indians.

## Mahatma Gandhi's legacy

**W**ho knows if young Mohandas *imagined* he would one day be a Mahatma? But the shy boy from Porbandar always *rose to his circumstances* – from the spelling test in Rajkot to opposing the injustice in South Africa to his multiple jail sentences in India, to leading one of the most *powerful independence movements* in modern history.

> "What I did was a
> VERY ORDINARY THING.
> I declared that the British
> COULD NOT ORDER ME AROUND
> in my own country."

Less than a hundred years ago, India was under the **brutal rule** of the British. Indian freedom has brought many successes, though there are still *challenges* to overcome. But it wouldn't have been possible without Mahatma Gandhi and the many others who *dedicated their lives* to the freedom movement.

Gandhi never preached what he couldn't follow himself. He was *supported* by his wife, Kasturba, who participated in the Satyagraha movements in South Africa and in India. Many of Gandhi's children and grandchildren lived in the Ashram, participated in the movement and *continue to practice his teachings*.

Mahatma Gandhi led an *extraordinary life* – as an active leader of peace, a social reformer, a writer, a self-taught nurse and dietician. Since his death in 1948 many world leaders like Nelson Mandela and Martin Luther King Jr., who fought for justice and freedom from oppression, have drawn inspiration from his teachings and applied satyagraha in their protests.

But to many in India, he is just *Bapu*, a fatherly figure who *set an example* for speaking the truth, being peaceful and living a simple but extraordinary life.

# TIMELINE

## 1869
Born on October 2 in Porbandar.

## 1883
Marries Kasturba.

## 1888
His first son Harilal is born, and Gandhi leaves for England to become a barrister.

## 1893
Arrives in South Africa.

Mahatma Gandhi

## 1894
Sets up Natal Indian Congress.

## 1919

Massacre at Jallianwala Bagh by General Dyer causes devastation. Gandhi decides that India needs complete independence from Britain.

## 1917

Sets up Sabarmati Ashram.

## 1918

First World War ends.

## 1914

Leaves South Africa.
First World War breaks out.

## 1913

Satyagraha campaign in South Africa against the Black Act.

## 1911

Delhi becomes the capital of British India.

## 1920

Noncooperation movement launched in India by Gandhi and the Indian National Congress.

## 1929

India declares itself free.

## 1930

India declares independence from the British and Gandhi sets off on Dandi March to break the Salt Act.

## 1931

Travels to England for negotiations.

## 1942

Gandhi and other leaders are arrested again.

## 1948

Gandhi is shot just before an evening prayer meeting and dies with a prayer on his lips. He is cremated by his sons on the bank of the River Yamuna.

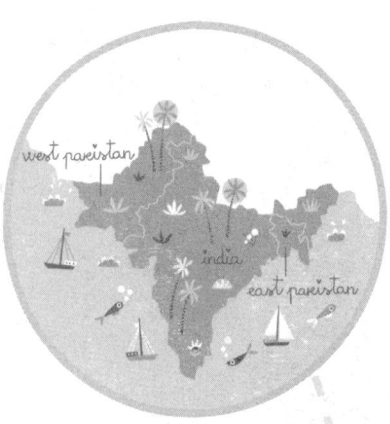

## 1947

Indian Independence Act is enacted in British Parliament; India partitioned and Pakistan created.

## 1944

Kasturba dies in jail in Gandhi's arms.

# SOME THINGS TO THINK ABOUT

Why do you think Mahatma Gandhi decided to protest peacefully, instead of using violence? Can you think of any other peaceful protests that have been successful, throughout history or in your own life?

Gandhi dedicated his life to trying to right what he saw as injustice in the world. Can you think of something happening in the world today that would inspire you to speak up for change?

Gandhi worked hard in South Africa fighting for the rights of Indian people. But when he was in South Africa, it wasn't just Indian people who were oppressed – racism affected all nonwhite people. In fact, in 1948 South Africa introduced *apartheid*, a system of racial segregation that enforced the oppression of people of color.

Have you heard of Nelson Mandela? He was a revolutionary political leader who worked to dismantle the oppressive system of apartheid in South Africa, becoming the country's first black President in 1994.

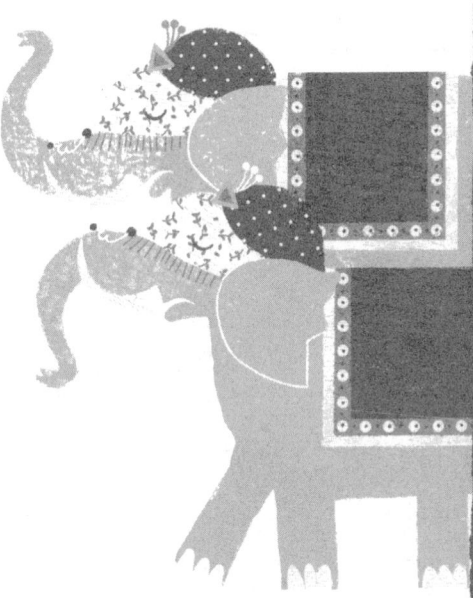

# Index

# Quote Sources

All quotes throughout are taken from *An Autobiography or The Story of My Experiments with Truth* (M. K. Gandhi, Navajivan Trust, 1927) except the following:

pp.80, 114: *A Week with Gandhi* (L. Fisher, Normanby Press, 1942)

pp.84–85, 87, 89, 92: *India of My Dreams*, (M. K. Gandhi, Navajivan Trust, 1947)